PERSONAL
DEVELOPMENT
SERIES

DECADE BY DECADE

LIFE IS SURPRISINGLY PREDICTABLE

**Maximizing This
Phase of Your Life**

Published by Aylen Publishing
7830 E. Camelback Road, Ste. 711
Scottsdale, AZ 85251
ISBN: 978-0-9910084-2-1

6th Printing

Written for

Advisors
Athletic Coaches
Attorneys
Board Members
Caregivers
Consultants
Counselors
Doctors
Educators
Entrepreneurs
Executive Team Members
Friends
Life Coaches
Managers
Mentors
Parents
Pastors
Presidents
Scout Leaders
Students of Life

Understanding life's predictabilities!

THE ELEPHANT STORY

As you are getting ready for the next decade of your life, remember this short story.

It was 11 o'clock one Friday night, and I was sound asleep when the phone rang. On the other end was my friend Duane Pederson, founder of the *Hollywood Free Paper*. "How would you like to go to Tucson tomorrow?"

"Tucson?" I groaned. "What in the world would we do in Tucson?"

"My friend, Bobby Yerkes, has a circus playing in Tucson tomorrow and I would like to just go down, get away, clear the cobwebs, and work the circus with him. We'll move some props, have a good time, and be back by 10 o'clock tomorrow night."

Now there probably isn't a boy alive who hasn't dreamed about running away with the circus as a child, so it didn't take me long to agree to go.

The next morning at 7 o'clock, our jet lifted off the runway at Los Angeles International Airport, headed for Tucson.

When we got there, it was a hot, dusty, windy day at

the fairgrounds where the circus was playing.

We moved props from one of the three rings to the next, helped in any way we could, and generally got dusty, dirty, tired, and hungry.

During one of the breaks, I started chatting with a man who trains animals for Hollywood movies. "How is it that you can stake down a 10-ton elephant with the same size stake that you use for this little fellow?" I asked, gesturing toward a baby elephant. (The "little fellow" weighed about 300 pounds.)

"It's easy when you know two things: elephants really do have great memories, but they really aren't very smart. When they are babies, we stake them down. They try to tug away from the stake maybe 10,000 times before they realize that they can't possibly get away. At that point, their elephant memory takes over and they remember for the rest of their lives that they can't get away from the stake."

We humans are sometimes like elephants. When we are teenagers, someone says, "He's not very handsome, she's not very pretty, they're not very good leaders," and zap! We drive a mental stake into our minds. Often, when we become full adults, we are still held back by some inaccurate, one-sentence "stake" put in our minds when we were years younger.

It is my hope that this story can help you pull up some of those stakes that are holding you back. Today you are an adult capable of much more than even you realize. You are more mature and capable than you were even 12 months ago, and next year you will be able to do things you can't today.

Let's pull up some stakes together!

Bob

DECADE by DECADE

UNDERSTANDING EACH DECADE OF LIFE

TABLE OF CONTENTS

THE ELEPHANT STORY   6

INTRODUCTION   15

1. CHILDREN UNDER 10 — **SECURITY** 21
   Am I LOVED and SAFE?

- Loving children unconditionally helps them build life confidence.

- Maximizing age 9/fourth grade, one of life's most shaping years.

- Helping each child connect actions and consequences.

2. TEENS — SELF   27
   What does any of it mean to ME?

   •   Visiting a mission,
       seeing others with less.

   •   Getting ready
       to leave home.

   •   Seeing the pitfalls
       of marrying before you are 25.

3. 20s — SURVIVAL   31
   Can I SURVIVE in the adult world?

   •   Relaxing — no one is expecting you
       to change the world in your 20s.

   •   Deciding what you do not want to do
       for the rest of your life!

   •   Saving ___% of your income and
       living on the rest.

4. **30s — SUCCESS**   37

   How SUCCESSFUL can I become?

   - Defining success,
     defining failure.

   - Balancing your time,
     family and work.

   - Finding a mentor
     and becoming one.

5. **40s — SIGNIFICANCE**   47

   *I'm successful, but is any of my
   work/life SIGNIFICANT?*

   - Moving your focus
     from success to significance.

   - Defining your lifework.

   - Struggling in our 40s is very normal!

6. 50s — STRIDE   61
      Am I "OVER THE HILL"?

  • Moving from "feeling old" to
     "getting ready" to maximize your 60s!

  • Defining your "north star."

  • Writing out
     your life milestones.

7. 60s — STRATEGIC   69
      How do I FINISH WELL?

  • Maximizing your most productive decade:
     your 60s.

  • Thinking strategically.

  • Moving from "full speed"
     to "semi-retirement."

8. 70s — **SUCCESSION**   79
    WHO will carry on what I've been doing?

- Mentoring your successors —
  a significant part of your legacy.

- Writing out your memories
  for the next 10 generations of your family.

- Keeping your will updated.

9. 80s — **SLIPPERY**   85
    Can I count on my HEALTH?

- Keeping up your health
  becomes a regular routine.

- Attending friends' funerals,
  supporting their family members.

- Reducing your expenses
  to a "new normal."

10. 90s-PLUS — SLEEP   91
    How long before I get to "SLEEP"?

- Telling your new young friends
  to call you by your first name.

- Selecting an advocate.

- Going to "sleep" in peace,
  preparing for your own passing.

WRAP UP   107

QUICK WISDOM   109

HELPING YOU ...   111

INTRODUCTION

HOW OLD WILL YOU BE IN 10 YEARS?

Sounds old, doesn't it?

Would it be helpful to you to have a broader life perspective on where you have been, where you are now, and where you are going? Would you like to understand where you are going based on the 40-plus years of patterns I've seen in my consulting with over 5,000 executives at different ages over an estimated 50,000 hours?

This is a quick-read book (no one has time to read 500 pages on very many subjects these days) that contains those observations and perspectives. These simple insights can be helpful to you — and anyone you meet — for the rest of your life!

"S-WORDS" HELP YOU RELAX

Here is a quick peek at the "S-WORD" FOCUS for each decade of life via one single word:

1. *CHILDREN UNDER 10* — **SECURITY.**
2. *TEENS* — **SELF.**
3. *20s* — **SURVIVAL.**
4. *30s* — **SUCCESS.**
5. *40s* — **SIGNIFICANCE/STRUGGLE.**
6. *50s* — **STRIDE.**
7. *60s* — **STRATEGIC.**
8. *70s* — **SUCCESSION.**
9. *80s* — **SLIPPERY.**
10. *90s-PLUS* — **SLEEP.**

All planning, personal and organizational, begins with an invisible phrase: "at this phase of life."

Your personal planning when you are 21 and single is different from when you are 31 with children, or 51 and an empty nester, or 91 in an assisted-living residence.

Understanding each phase of life helps you relax and breathe a very real sigh of relief at very deep emotional levels, and realize that what you are experiencing is somewhat normal.

You will gain PERSPECTIVE on each decade, making it easy to envision yourself and others and be a quick reference for the future. We'll start each chapter with a SINGLE-WORD FOCUS and a KEY QUESTION (i.e., the unconscious, emotionally disturbing question of that decade).

This instantly gives you a 50,000-foot-level view of each decade. Then I'll share with you ideas to maximize each decade. These ideas will help strategically focus your thinking for each decade.

Simply understanding the SINGLE-WORD FOCUS for each decade also gives you a tool to quickly remember, and deeply understand, the emotional world of those family members, friends, and team members who are younger and older than you.

YOU ARE NOT ALONE

For the past 45-plus years I have been teaching clients "nothing is meaningful without context." Understanding the context that you and your friends are in also gives you a context far broader than just today's pressures.

These ideas help you gain a far deeper understanding of what others are experiencing, so you can explain, "You are not alone, and it is OK to be exactly where you are." Explain that their feelings are predictable and normal.

With predictability comes a new level of confidence to face the future they are facing. It removes the unnecessary pressure that always accompanies unrealistic expectations ("Where I should be ... thought I would be ... others thought I would be") at a particular phase of life.

Once you realize you are not alone in experiencing what you are experiencing, you begin developing realistic expectations of where you are (not where you "should" be) at this phase of life. Most people — including most of my clients and friends — breathe a deep sigh of relief and actually begin to relax!

Muscle relaxer pills help you
RELAX for an **HOUR physically**.

Life perspective helps you
RELAX for a **DECADE emotionally**!

Relax does not mean you get lazy. Relax does not mean you stop working. Relax does not mean you lose all motivation. It simply means the pressure you feel to perform is dramatically reduced and you can relax emotionally.

In this book you will discover how to start relaxing at a far deeper level in this phase of your life. You will:

- Gain perspective on where you are in life.

- Learn how to help others in each decade of their lives.

- Deepen your understanding of others in your professional world.

- Learn how to answer questions like, "Why would they be feeling this or that?"

The observations and perspectives in this book strike most people as very good news. You will find in it fresh, healthy, encouraging perspectives. Hopefully, you will be helping a friend with these ideas before this week (or day) has ended.

Chapter 1: Children Under 10

Word of the decade:

Security

Unconscious, emotionally disturbing question of the decade:

AM I LOVED AND SAFE?

LOVING CHILDREN UNCONDITIONALLY HELPS THEM BUILD LIFE CONFIDENCE

If you are a person who works with children, you know children crave unconditional love. Tell them often, "I love you. I will always love you, no matter what you do or don't do." Being loved without conditions gives children a deep sense of life security.

Children experience love emotionally at levels they can't put into words.

- TRULY LOVED: Without conditions.

- INCONSISTENTLY LOVED: Imagine a child with a parent who is very loving when sober and cruel when under the influence of drugs, alcohol, or other severe mood swings. The child experiences this as "If he/she doesn't love me all of the time I'm not really loved at all." Unloved; not worthy of being loved.

- CONDITIONALLY LOVED: Imagine a child who reads between the lines from the parent: "If you get B's I love you, but if you got straight A's I'd love you more!" The child internalizes that as: "I'm not really loved at all; I'm unloved ... not worthy of being loved."

- UNLOVED: Imagine a child who feels no love at all; who feels unloved and totally unworthy of love. You would be surprised at the number of adults with whom I have discussed these levels of love who confess to feeling zero love in their childhood.

Confidence is a byproduct of predictability in all areas of life.

This concept applies to (and can be helpful in) all phases of life. However, it is shaped primarily in the elementary school years.

TWO LEVELS OF CONFIDENCE:

- SITUATIONAL CONFIDENCE.
  Your child may be very confident only in one specific area (e.g., playing baseball); when doing anything else he/she feels very insecure.

- LIFE CONFIDENCE.
  If your child has received unconditional love they tend to be flexible, comfortable in almost any situation, and have life confidence.

If confidence is lacking in any area of her/his (or your) life, don't try to pump up confidence; simply restore predictability, and confidence returns as a natural byproduct.

MAXIMIZING AGE 9/FOURTH GRADE, ONE OF LIFE'S MOST SHAPING YEARS

What you're comfortable doing today, as an adult, is what you were comfortable doing when you were 9. If you weren't comfortable doing it at 9, chances are you aren't really relaxed and comfortable doing it today.

If you have a 9-year-old (daughter, son, granddaughter, grandson, niece, nephew, neighborhood child, etc.) in your life, see this as a unique phase of life to spend a disproportionate amount of time together, because all of their adult comfort zones are being shaped in this year!

Protect your 9-year-olds at all costs. Get them out of schools, social groups, friendships, etc., if they are mistreated there. Have them play with both older and younger children to teach them to both lead and follow. Find your fourth-grader's favorite "talk time" and be available to listen. In addition to nicknames, give every child a "heart name" (used only to address that child, and only when you're alone with her/him).

This is not the place to go into detail about age 9. See the *4th Grade(r)* book or DVD at BobbBiehl.com if you are specifically interested in the fourth-grade phase of life.

HELPING EACH CHILD CONNECT
ACTIONS AND CONSEQUENCES

The fourth grade is also the critical time for making sure each child you care about understands the very real cause-and-effect relationship between actions and consequences.

Make it clear:

> If you do A, then B is the result.
> If you do *not* do A, then C is the result.

This is the relationship so many teenagers do not clearly understand, which breaks the hearts of so many parents.

Having a very clear sense of rewards and punishments is one of the keys to a child having a deep sense of a predictable world in which to feel very secure.

REMEMBER:

Give every child you care about
a deep sense of love and SECURITY!

CHAPTER 2: TEENS

Word of the decade:

Self

Unconscious, emotionally disturbing question of the decade:

WHAT DOES IT MEAN TO ME?

By now, you have likely seen thousands of hours of TV, movies, videos, etc. In most of those thousands of hours, the "screen teen" looks perfect and seems endlessly rich.

It is never spelled out on the screen that they have been in an offscreen makeup room for hours with professional makeup artists and don't always personally have every single thing money can buy.

This puts you in the position of comparing yourself and feeling, "I'm poor, ugly, and 'deprived' of a new sports car, the latest high-fashion clothes, and all things good at this phase of my life."

VISITING A MISSION:
SEEING OTHERS WITH LESS

At this point in life it is really helpful for you to go visit a mission (local or foreign) to help gain life perspective, by seeing how really deprived people live in very humble circumstances.

One trip can entirely change your perspective on whether what you do has meaning. It is helpful to see everyone is not beautiful, rich, driving the latest cars at top speed, and wearing the very latest designer fashions. To go on a mission trip adds a world perspective very quickly.

Another benefit of going on a mission trip is that you are asked on the mission trip to GIVE, GIVE, GIVE, not to just GET, GET, GET! Instead of feeling like you always have less than others (on TV), it shows you that in the real world you have far more than most.

GETTING READY TO LEAVE HOME

Your teen years are also the time when you are sometimes putting on a mask: "Nothing scares me." Yet inside, you are asking, "Am I really ready to leave home? Am I ready to be off on my own?" You're also wondering, "How do I survive in the mean, cruel, costly world just beyond my parents' home? Can I make it in college? Can I get/keep a job?" You are going to make it, just as millions have before you.

By the way, many teenagers assume that the day they turn 18 they are then adults. They want to be treated like adults. Don't let that artificial threshold put mega pressure on you, like it does many teens. There are more than just two phases of growing up:

CHILD → Age 18 → ADULT

There are actually three phases:

CHILD → Age 18 → STUDENT → ADULT

Society doesn't typically see you as an adult until you are 25 or so — not until you can hold a job, make consistent car payments, live on your own, and establish your own credit.

You may want to read a copy of my book *On My Own,* written specifically for those getting ready to be on their own for the first time! It offers many principles for handling real life beyond your parents' threshold. It is also a great book to use in discussion of those proven principles with your parents. (See BobbBiehl.com.)

SEEING THE PITFALLS
OF MARRYING BEFORE YOU ARE 25

Whatever you do, don't plan to get married until you are at least 25 years old. The change rate in the late teen years and early 20s is amazing. Let's say you get married when you are 19; by the time you're 23, you're a different person — and so is the person you married! One of the reasons we have so many people divorcing in their later 20s is because they often marry someone when they're 19; then, by the time they're 23, I hear, "We don't have anything in common anymore!" Both have changed so much.

May I suggest that you set a target of age 25 as a great time to begin considering marriage? As a reality check, every single couple my daughter knew who got married before age 22 were divorced by the time they were 30. That doesn't necessarily mean that would be the case with you, but it is a real fact.

You are in the process of learning, growing, getting ready — RELAX!

Chapter 3: **20s**

Word of the decade:

SURVIVAL

Unconscious, emotionally disturbing question of the decade:

CAN I SURVIVE IN THE ADULT WORLD?

RELAX — NO ONE IS EXPECTING YOU TO CHANGE THE WORLD IN YOUR 20s.

Do you ever think, "Everyone in the world is watching me"? Do you ever feel you are going to disappoint everyone who has invested in you because you don't have a perfect job? You know what? No one's watching you. Your mom and dad are, but that's about it. No one really expects anything of you yet. They don't expect you to change the world yet. Relax! When people ask what you are going to do now that you're out of school, they aren't really holding you responsible for changing the world quite yet. They simply don't know what else to ask. Relax!

DECIDING WHAT YOU DO *NOT* WANT TO DO FOR THE REST OF YOUR LIFE!

You may be feeling a tremendous amount of pressure. You may be thinking the world is going to end if you don't decide today what you're going to do for the rest of your life, and if you don't make it happen in the next year or two.

NO, NO, NO! What you're trying to decide right now is what you don't want to do for the rest of your life. The greatest mistake is not being 21 years old and not knowing what you want to do the rest of your life. Your greatest mistake is being 21 and making the wrong decision and being stuck there when you're 37 with three children, two cars, and a huge mortgage. If you don't know what you want to do until age 35 or 40, it's still not too late to settle on a different career.

An exception is a profession demanding much post-graduate education, such as medicine.

Try something you really enjoy that pays your bills for a year. If you think you want to go into accounting, go into accounting. Try it for a year or so. If you like it, stay another year.

If you don't like it, GET OUT!

If it is your dream, try being part of a rock band. If you don't like that, try sales, bus driving, the building trades, or whatever you think you may want to do.

Try a wide variety of professions in your 20s —
anything you think you may want to do for the rest of
your life.

You likely feel a fair amount of pressure to settle down
on something, right? I respond, "No, no, no!" As long
as you are paying your own way, until you are in your
30s just relax. What you're hoping is that by the time
you're 30, you'll find it.

Parents, you need to relax a little bit too with your
young adults in their 20s.

SAVING ___% OF YOUR INCOME, LIVING ON THE REST

Alert: You may have been watching your parents
for years "living the good life," putting everything
on credit cards and saving nothing. But when your
parents hit an economic downturn, you saw them
under tremendous economic pressure, or even
possibly bankrupt.

A very wealthy man once taught me: Save X percent
(you decide the percentage today and stay with it for
the next 50 years or so) of whatever you make first,
and live on the rest. Let your lifestyle follow your
savings. If you establish your lifestyle and then save
what's left, there will never be any left.

Put your savings in a jar, put it in stocks, put it in a bank — set it aside for the future. It is there for true emergencies and moneymaking opportunities.

One hundred percent of the young leaders in their 20s that I've shared this idea with have responded, "That really makes sense — thank you!" When I share the idea with older leaders, they unanimously say, "I wish someone had told me that when I was in my 20s."

You are BECOMING AN ADULT ...
your most productive decade will be your 60s
... RELAX AND ENJOY THE RIDE!

WHERE DO I GO FROM HERE?

If you are like most readers, you skipped chapters to quickly learn about your current decade. That's fine!

Does what you have read "hit the nail on the head," as most readers say?
If it does, where do you go from here?

May I suggest one of five steps:

1. Read the *rest* of the book
   ... to anticipate more and more of your own future.

2. **Read *earlier* chapters**
   ... to better understand what your children and protégés are feeling.

3. **Read about a decade someone you care *about* is in today**
   ... to help you better understand her/his current phase of life.

4. **Read and *give* your book to a family member or friend**
   ... to help them better understand their life situation at this time.

5. **Read and file this book in your personal *library***
   ... to reread when you get to each of your next decades.

You
are in a very different phase of life today
than you were 10 years ago
or will be 10 years from now!

Happy to get a few pages to think with you about this phase of your life!

Bobb

Chapter 4: **30s**

Word of the decade:

SUCCESS

*Unconscious, emotionally disturbing question
of the decade:*

HOW SUCCESSFUL CAN I BECOME?

DEFINING SUCCESS
DEFINING FAILURE

By the time you hit your 30s, your "S" word is
SUCCESS.

You are focused on trying to figure out answers to
questions like: "How SUCCESSFUL can I become?
How far can I go up the ladder? How much money
can I make? How many promotions can I get? How
much money can I make by the time I'm 40?"

The focus of most young leaders in their 30s is
typically SUCCESS. Success is actually not defined
very clearly in the thinking of most thirty-somethings;
they just want to get wherever they are going as fast

as they can, go as high as they possibly can, and be a success!

Let me take just a minute here to chat with you about success.

1. Young leaders in their 30s often unconsciously think of success as a destination: "becoming a millionaire," "becoming president of my company," or "being at the top of my profession."

   When they reach those destinations, when asked if they believe they are now successful, the most common answer I hear is, "I don't really know."

   The person who sets a goal of making a million dollars a year but only makes $900,000 will feel far less successful than a person who sets a goal of making $90,000 but actually makes $100,000.

2. The feeling of success comes from having what you want, and/or wanting what you have.

   When you focus on being thankful for what you have today, you will feel far more successful than you would wanting something you will never achieve.

   You may push back a bit, saying, "But if I focus on already feeling successful with what I have and enjoying it, doesn't that take the future incentive out of my life?" No, it can take two things to make you happy: what you have, and having a plan for tomorrow. When you have milestones and a plan, you feel happy and successful.

You have known many people who don't make nearly as much money as you, yet feel very successful compared to their past, or to other people, or to their own dreams.

You have known others who have made far more than you, perhaps, but who don't seem to feel very successful at all.

3. The feeling of success keeps changing with the aging process.

    Success is a galloping feeling. When you make a consistent $100,000 per year, soon you won't feel as successful as the person making $125,000. What you considered very successful last year will seem far less successful next year. What is successful to a 31-year-old may seem like hardly scratching the surface of success to a 40-, 50- or 60-year-old.

One more time: success is simply a feeling. It keeps changing. It is not a destination where one day you will say to yourself, "I am now successful!"

What then is failure?

Failure, too, is simply a feeling. It is the reverse of success.

1. Failure is simply a feeling, not a destination.

2. The feeling of failure comes from not having what you want, and/or having what you *don't* want.

3. The feeling of failure keeps changing with the aging process. What may seem like success to a 30-year-old may feel like failure to a 50-year-old.

BALANCING YOUR TIME: FAMILY AND WORK

If you are in your 30s, ask yourself, "At this phase of my life — realistically, with the children I have, with the finances I have, with the total life I have — how much time do I need to get away on vacation, to clear my head, to keep my balance, to reflect on the future, to reflect on the past?" How much time at this phase of life do you need to spend time with your parents, assuming they are still living? Because you're not guaranteed how long they will be alive.

Get comfortable using terms like "death," "die," and "dead," because they're reality. If your parents are still living today, but you somehow knew they would not be living next year, how much time would you wish you had spent with them this year?

Plan your breaks a year in advance.

Most young people in their 30s tend to be so intent on success that they lose balance. They work 80-hour weeks and their family never sees them. You've got plenty of time left in life to achieve success; find some balance here.

Learn how to balance home and business priorities by planning a year in advance. Create an Annual Balance Calendar by drawing a circle with 1 to 12 marked around the circumference (like the hours on a clock), representing months. Pencil in your fixed (year after year) time blocks (your busy seasons and your slow seasons), appointments, the breaks you'd like to take, personal retreats, family visits, etc. Then transfer these dates into your "this year" calendar.

Annual Balance Calendar

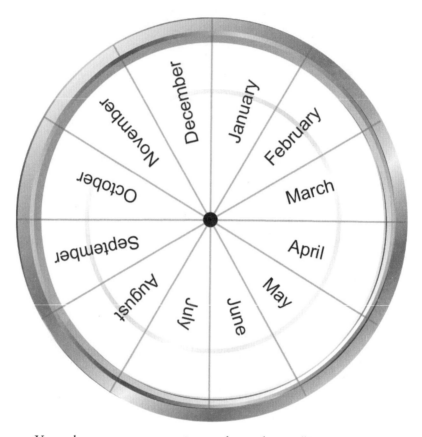

Yesterday, a young executive spoke with me. "I wanna work hard until I'm 60, then I want to take a break," he said confidently. "My wife and I want to take a break and travel." When hearing this kind of limited perspective from a 30- to 40-year-old, I say, "No one guarantees you age 40. No one. No one is guaranteed tomorrow. Take your breaks with your spouse, children, and parents NOW!"

Also, if you don't schedule it a year in advance, there's never a good time to take a break.

Imagine if I told you, "You have to take next week off!" You would most likely say, "Bobb, you don't understand. I've got appointments all next week!"

Do you know the only reason you can't take off next week? You didn't put it on your yearly calendar a year ago and make your schedule around next week. All the people you are meeting with next week would have been happy to meet you this week, or the week after next, if they knew you were going to be out of town next week.

You can take breaks. You just have to schedule them a year in advance, and this advanced scheduling is what allows you to keep your annual balance. You need to have annual balance, not just daily or weekly balance.

You may respond, "Bobb, I just can't do that at this phase of my life."

If this is your response, you will be putting off a balanced planning process when you are in your 80s. At this point, you may not be able to take as much time as you want, have as much money as you want, or be able to go any place in the world. But you can take some time, with some money, to go someplace, knowing as time goes by, decade by decade, you will likely be able to take more and more.

(*The Annual Balance Calendar* is a segment of the *Leadership Academy* video series found at BobbBiehl. com.)

FINDING A MENTOR AND BECOMING ONE

One of the finest ways I've ever seen to accelerate your success in life is to find the right mentor(s)!

> Ideally, mentoring is a lifelong relationship in which a mentor helps a protégé reach their God-given potential.

Who are the two or three wisest people you know personally — people you like, believe in, and look up to? Ask one of those two or three individuals, "Would you consider being one of my life mentors?" Be careful. Don't say, "Would you consider being my mentor?" That seems too heavy a responsibility. Instead ask, "Would you consider being one of my mentors?"

You are going to run into a lot of situations where you are going to need objective, experienced wisdom. Having a mentor is one of the best possible ways to accelerate progress toward SUCCESS!

It's shocking the number of young leaders in their 30s who don't have a parent they feel they can go to for wise counsel.

At the same time, consider becoming a mentor to someone you believe in who is younger and less experienced than you at this point in life.

(For a far more complete discussion of the mentoring relationship, see *Mentoring: How to Find a Mentor and How to Become One* at BobbBiehl.com.)

You can accelerate your success
and maximize your life balance in all areas
by FINDING THE RIGHT MENTOR!

WHERE DO I GO FROM HERE?

If you are like most readers, you skipped chapters to quickly learn about your current decade. That's fine!

Does what you have read "hit the nail on the head," as most readers say?
If it does, where do you go from here?

May I suggest one of five steps:

1. Read the *rest* of the book
... to anticipate more and more of your own future.

2. **Read *earlier* chapters**
    ... to better understand what your children and protégés are feeling.

3. **Read about a decade someone you care *about* is in today**
    ... to help you better understand her/his current phase of life.

4. **Read and *give* your book to a family member or friend**
    ... to help them better understand their life situation at this time.

5. **Read and file this book in your personal *library***
    ... to reread when you get to each of your next decades.

You
are in a very different phase of life today
than you were 10 years ago
or will be 10 years from now!

Happy to get a few pages to think with you about this phase of your life!

Bob

CHAPTER 5: **40s**

Word of the decade:

SIGNIFICANCE

Unconscious, emotionally disturbing question of the decade:

I'M SUCCESSFUL, BUT IS MY WORK SIGNIFICANT?

MOVING YOUR FOCUS FROM SUCCESS TO SIGNIFICANCE

Are you wrestling with the topic of significance?

In your 30s you were more than likely very successful, but somewhere between 37 and 43 your question begins to change. Instead of asking, "Am I successful?" you ask, "Is what I'm doing making any significant difference?"

But what is significance?

SIGNIFICANCE is making a difference that lasts over time. The longer the difference lasts, the more significant the activity feels.

DEFINING YOUR LIFEWORK

What would you enjoy doing for the rest of your life?

When we hit "the big 4-0," we say to ourselves, "I'm 40, halfway to 80. Could I see myself doing what I'm doing for the rest of my life?" Often, the answer is, "No way! But what else do I want to do?"

One day, while talking to a high-visibility client, I casually asked him one of my all-time favorite questions: "How goes the battle?"

When you ask this of someone, they might answer, "Fine, great, never better." Or they may answer, "Things are really heavy at the moment." This question gives you a super quick emotional pulse check.

When I asked it of my 42-year-old client, he said, "Oh, I'm doing pretty well. I'm not in a midlife crisis or anything, but I am deep in a midlife reevaluation." A midlife reevaluation is an emotionally healthy, positive thing to do between the ages of 37 and 43. Ask yourself, "Could I see myself doing what I'm doing professionally for the rest of my life?" These are the ages where a person is old enough to "know what they know" and young enough to make a change into something they would prefer doing for the rest of their life.

You might be wrestling with questions like these: "Am I in the right career? Have I got the right job? Am I in the right profession?" If so, and your answer is a resounding, "I don't know!" then let me give you a word your instincts are looking for today: lifework. Your instincts are looking for a significant — i.e., making a major difference over time — lifework.

> Your lifework
> is the work you could see yourself doing
> for the rest of your life.

You may say, "That's it, that's what I've been looking for the past few months/years." If you haven't found your lifework by the time you're 40, and you feel it is very important to do so, today is a good time to start looking for it.

Some of my Christian clients have responded, "I just want to do what God wants me to do." This response is very noble and commendable. But you may have been resting in this position for years and still "hear" no clear sense of direction.

In my experience, God often feels very silent on the subject of your lifework. What if you reverse your prayer? What if you pray, "God, if you have in your mind any specific thing you want me to do, please make crystal clear that it is You speaking and I'll do whatever you ask of me." This is what I would call "committing your way to the Lord."

Scripture is very clear: "Commit your ways to the Lord, that he may give you the desires of your heart." What if God were to tell you, "You have committed yourself to Me ... therefore, you are free to choose"?

If God doesn't seem to be leading in a given direction, how would you decide your next steps?

Ask yourself this one question that I've asked myself and others more than 500 times:

> If I could do anything I wanted,
> if I had all the time, money, staff, and education I needed,
> and God told me, "You are free to choose,"
> and
> if I knew for certain I couldn't fail,
> what would I do?

What would be your answer?

What makes you weep or pound the table?
Often this one question helps clear the fog as well.

Why spend the rest of your life doing something you don't really care that much about?
One more bit of fog-cutting advice that many clients have found freeing:

> Decide where you want to grow old,
> move there as soon as you can,
> find work there,

make all the friends you can,
and
die among friends.

Do this
instead of living where you don't want to live,
doing what you don't want to do,
growing old there,
and moving to a retirement community in a
warmer climate
and
dying among strangers.

Make sense to you?

In the process of defining your lifework, define your
single greatest strength:

Of all the things you do well, what do you do the
very best?

This is your SINGLE GREATEST STRENGTH!

These questions force your brain to summarize all
of those thoughts roaming around in your head and
come to a very focused conclusion. Sometimes it
helps in the process of defining your strength to put
your single greatest strength into a single word or
short phrase.

When you try to choose one single word, often you

come up with a word you don't initially understand; you've never heard anyone use this word to describe anyone before. The word I came up with was "conceptualist." I immediately understood the basic meaning of the word. Conceptualists create new, original concepts. I had heard of people being called teacher, professor, doctor, and lawyer, but "conceptualist"? I had never heard of a conceptualist!

One close friend told me, "Bobb, the only word that comes to my mind when I ask the question is 'piercer.'"

I said, "Hmm, interesting word. What does it mean?" In a slightly confused tone, he said, "I don't have a clue!" I encouraged him: "Well, think about it for a minute — what does it mean to you?"

In a mildly frustrated tone he said, "I don't know. All I know is that whenever a problem comes up I seem to have the ability to pierce right through the center of it!"

I looked at him and affirmed his choice: "Friend, you are a piercer!" Since then, for over a decade, whenever I've encountered a certain kind of problem I just can't seem to get my head around, I call him. He ignores all of my mental fog and goes right to the heart of the issue.

What word would you use about you? It's not too late if you're over 40 to ask the question; but if you're 40, now is certainly the time to ask the question, because what you're trying to do in your lifework is find alignment between three main elements.

What is my SINGLE GREATEST STRENGTH?
What do I do best?

What is my PASSION?
What do I feel deeply burdened by and uniquely qualified to do?

What is my DREAM?
What difference do I want to make before I die? (This can be your own dream, or a dream you're helping someone else realize.)

The point where these three elements are in alignment will point toward your lifework.

By the time you're 40, you should have also moved on from what other people think of you to what's going on inside of you. It doesn't matter what society thinks of you — it really does not. It matters what God and a few close friends think of you. What society thinks of you shouldn't matter at this phase of life. If you are a conceptualist, be a conceptualist. If you are a piercer, be a piercer. If you are a _____, be a _____.

There are certain areas in which you will be a star. In other areas, even if you tried very hard, you'd be a dismal failure. That's just life. As Dr. Peter F. Drucker once told me,

> "The role of an organization is to maximize the strength of the individual and make her or his weakness irrelevant."

What you're trying to do is combine your STRENGTHS, DREAM, and PASSION into your LIFEWORK and MAXIMIZE it!

In what we choose for our lifework, our weakness should be irrelevant. The fact that I can't play basketball is, in fact, irrelevant to my consulting practice. There are a lot of things you cannot do. Just because your dad could do them, or your mom could do them, or your aunt or uncle or famous grandpa or grandma could do them, DOES NOT MEAN you can do them — or should even try.

By the second half of our 40s, we begin to abandon activities we no longer want to do at all!
By the last half of our 40s, we have decided where we are strong, where we are weak, what we want our lifework to be — and, therefore, what we want to stop even trying as soon as possible! These are things we DO NOT WANT TO DO!

STRUGGLING IN OUR 40s IS VERY NORMAL!

Another word that is critical to understanding those in their 40s is STRUGGLE.

> It feels like you are a very strong,
> Kentucky Derby-level thoroughbred racehorse
> running through six inches of deep, wet mud.

> No matter how hard you try, it seems you can
> never get up to the speed of which you are
> capable!

The vast majority of 40- to 50-year-olds are struggling substantially in life. There are very few that I've met who have not agreed 100 percent with the emotional feeling of the racehorse description above.

They're struggling just to pay the bills, struggling with personal identity, struggling with children, or struggling with work. In my observations, the 40s is typically the toughest decade of all. Let me repeat: the toughest decade of all!

> You're no longer a whiz kid
> and yet
> you're not a whiz adult quite yet.
> You aren't what you will become,
> and yet
> you aren't what you used to be.

You're sort of stuck in the middle somewhere. That's

a painful process. It feels like the struggling will never end.

The unconscious or erroneous conclusion is, "This is the way adult life is. This is what it will feel like the rest of my life ... then I die!"

WRONG!

This is precisely how it feels, but it is not true! You are only in a phase of life that is seemingly without end. But when you hit your early 50s, it all changes. The racetrack begins to dry out, your speed picks up, and your natural energy begins to return. You begin to hit your stride!

In dealing with literally hundreds of executives in their 40s, both female and male, I've noticed one very specific struggle that deserves a spotlight.

Most people in their 40s make one dangerous and incorrect unconscious assumption:

"By the time I'm fortysomething, I should be rich!"

WRONG!

But those in their 40s typically don't yet understand this reality. They do not have perspective on their unconscious pressure to be "rich." In fact, they are feeling like underachievers, because they unconsciously believe they should be rich by now!

Help anyone you know in their 40s understand one very simple — and very freeing — truth. If you are in your 40s, listen carefully! A few years ago, a highly reputable financial magazine did a survey and asked the "super rich,"

"In what decade of your life did you make the most money?"

A very high percentage of those in their 40s answer with reflective sadness, "In their 40s, probably."

The actual answer is their 60s.

Most super wealthy people made most of their money in their 60s, not in their 40s. The second decade in which they made lots of money was their 70s — not their 40s. The third decade in which they made the most money was their 50s, not their 40s.

The 40s don't even show up!

If you are in your 40s and you can pay your rent, pay your mortgage, make your car payments, pay for your kids' school, buy their school clothes, and deal with them needing "new tennis shoes every other week" as they grow, then you're way ahead of most in their 40s!

Feel the relief?

I can't tell you the relief that comes to the emotional systems of those in their 40s when they hear this simple truth. The most typical response I get from those in their 40s is a lung-deep sigh of relief — often followed by, "I can't wait to tell my spouse!"

Be very careful in your 40s not to compare yourself to those in their 60s. It will get you depressed for no good reason. They are in a very different phase from you!

Is this making sense to you?

REMEMBER

In your 40s, you are defining your strengths and your lifework. This is normally the toughest decade of life. It feels like this struggling is going to last forever.

The good news?

IT DOESN'T!

WHERE DO I GO FROM HERE?

If you are like most readers, you skipped chapters to quickly learn about your current decade. That's fine!

Does what you have read "hit the nail on the head," as most readers say?

If it does, where do you go from here?

May I suggest one of five steps:

1. Read the *rest* of the book
   ... to anticipate more and more of your own future.

2. Read *earlier* chapters
   ... to better understand what your children and protégés are feeling.

3. Read about a decade someone you care *about* is in today
   ... to help you better understand her/his current phase of life.

4. Read and *give* your book to a family member or friend
   ... to help them better understand their life situation at this time.

5. Read and file this book in your personal *library*
   ... to reread when you get to each of your next decades.

You
are in a very different phase of life today
than you were 10 years ago
or will be 10 years from now!

Happy to get a few pages to think with you about this
phase of your life!

Bob

Chapter 6: **50s**

Word of the decade:

STRIDE

Unconscious, emotionally disturbing question of the decade:

AM I "OVER THE HILL"?

Finally, by the time you hit your early 50s, the struggles of the 40s typically begin to let up a bit.

Like I said earlier, in your 40s you felt like you were a very strong, Kentucky Derby-level thoroughbred racehorse running through six inches of deep, wet mud. No matter how hard you tried, it seemed you could never get up to the speed of which you were capable!

In your early 50s, the track begins to dry out! You can feel your speed picking up; you are beginning to hit your STRIDE!

You're getting traction. Every time you make a move, something happens. A lot of things start coming together in your 50s. Here is where you say to yourself,

> I know what I know!
> I know who I know!
> Everyone knows I know!
> I'm ready to go!

MOVING FROM "FEELING OLD" TO "GETTING READY" TO MAXIMIZE YOUR 60S!

Every person I have talked to between ages 50 and 53 has very quickly admitted to feeling "old" on certain days. This is when it occurs to you, "I'm halfway to my 100th birthday; statistically, my life is half over." You start paying even more attention to your health — that's why people in their 50s begin going on diets, joining health clubs, and getting more regular health checkups.

But remember what I said earlier: "Your 60s is the single most productive decade of your life!" You are far from "over the hill"! You are in the last decade of preparation to absolutely maximize your 60s. The profound question you ask yourself at this phase of life is:

> "What are the 10 measurable priorities
> I need to complete in my 50s to be exactly where I

want to be on my 60th birthday
to maximize the decade of my 60s?"

When most people in their early 50s hear this thought — that their best decade is actually their 60s — they typically take a deep breath and say something like, "I feel you have just given me a fresh start in life. I no longer feel over the hill; I feel I'm really just getting started in preparing for my 60s and my 70s!"

Our early 50s are usually a pleasurable time. This is when we often become empty nesters as the children go off to college or leave home in other ways, giving us more time for our own interests. This often leaves a bit more budget freedom, travel freedom, and freedom for life in general.

This is also a great phase of life to become a mentor. You have a bit more time for mentoring others and sharing the life wisdom/experience you have gained. It is still wise to have a mentor at this phase of your life as well.

(See the book *MENTORING: How to Find a Mentor and How to Become One* at BobbBiehl.com.)

DEFINING YOUR "NORTH STAR"

Your early 50s is a great time to review your "north star." Your personal north star is your 50,000-foot direction, not your destination. It is like the North Star in the sky; it is never your destination, but it gives you a sense of direction so you always know, "This way is north!"

Here are five points of your north star (take one single sentence to answer each question):

Top point:

WHO IS GOD?
(Your answer affects your entire life)

Top left point:

WHY AM I ON THIS EARTH?
(Your life purpose/mission)

Top right point:

WHAT DIFFERENCE DO I WANT TO MAKE BEFORE I LEAVE THIS EARTH?
(Your life dream/vision)

Bottom left point:

HOW WILL I MAKE THIS DIFFERENCE?
(Your lifework)

Bottom right point:

HOW LONG DO I WANT THIS DIFFERENCE TO LAST?
(Your legacy)

(A fuller *North Star* introductory video is part of the *Leadership Academy* DVD series available at BobbBiehl.com.)

It is a good idea to take a bit of time in your early 50s to reflect on, define, and clarify these five life-direction questions as a context for all of your other activities.

WRITING OUT YOUR LIFE MILESTONES

At the same time that you are looking forward with your purpose/mission statement, a fun, rewarding, perspective-bringing exercise to do in your early 50s is to make a list of your life milestones. This list helps you bring a positive perspective to the discouraging times everyone experiences. If you haven't made this list, I would encourage you to make a list of everything you've done right so far in life.

This is a list I have kept updated in my computer for the past 20 years. Do you know who has seen that list? No one — not even my wife, Cheryl. It's not that I'm trying to keep it from her, but this isn't a bragging list. It isn't a list that boasts to the world, "Look at all I've done!"

This is a list of the things you've done right so when you experience one of life's traumas, you can look at it to keep perspective. When you get in a tight spot, when you fail at something, when you get fired, when you get reprimanded, when you lose an account, when anything goes wrong, you can review the list and say to yourself, "This didn't go the way I wanted, but a lot of things in my life have gone right!" It gives you a far more balanced perspective in this phase of life.

You may also want to include on the list all of the major setbacks you have experienced and the positive lessons you have learned as a result. Major progress!

In your 50s, when you realize you are "not old,"
you start getting ready,
looking backward, and looking forward
to maximize your coming 60s!

WHERE DO I GO FROM HERE?

If you are like most readers, you skipped chapters to quickly learn about your current decade. That's fine!

Does what you have read "hit the nail on the head," as most readers say?

If it does, where do you go from here?

May I suggest one of five steps:

1. Read the *rest* of the book
... to anticipate more and more of your own future.

2. Read *earlier* chapters
... to better understand what your children and protégés are feeling.

3. Read about a decade someone you care *about* is in today
... to help you better understand her/his current phase of life.

4. Read and *give* your book to a family member or friend
... to help them better understand their life situation at this time.

5. Read and file this book in your personal *library*
... to reread when you get to each of your next decades.

You
are in a very different phase of life today
than you were 10 years ago
or will be 10 years from now!

Happy to get a few pages to think with you about this phase of your life!

Bob

CHAPTER 7: **60s**

Word of the decade:

STRATEGIC

Unconscious, emotionally disturbing question of the decade:

How do I FINISH WELL?

MAXIMIZING YOUR MOST PRODUCTIVE DECADE: YOUR 60s

Your 60s decade is typically the decade of greatest...

Income

> You have more income — and, typically, reduced expenses — giving you far more flexible spending money for travel and other enjoyable spending. Maximize it!

Networking

You know more people on your friends and
contacts list, have more real friends,
and are invited to more events than any other
decade. Maximize it!

Trust

Your network trusts you the most in your 60s —
not when you are in your 30s, 40s, or even your
50s. Maximize it!

Influence

Many of my clients have been guests on nationally
broadcast talk show programs more often in their
60s than in all previous decades put together.
It takes a certain amount of time to develop a
nationally respected organization, a credible
reputation, a strong network, a solid platform,
and a national impact/influence. Maximize it!

Expertise

You are the expert in your field. Maximize it!

THINKING STRATEGICALLY

We live our 60s in a delicate balance:

- realizing this is the most productive decade of our lives,

- and, at the same time, realizing fully that we are not promised tomorrow.

You will find that this combination causes you to have more strategic focus in your 60s than you have ever had in your life.

Here are 10 questions that can help you focus your thinking in very strategic directions. Answer each with one sentence:

- Why am I on earth?

- What is my unique/single greatest strength?
  How can I maximize it?

- What do I never tire of doing?
  How can I maximize this activity?

- If I could do
    three things in the next
    90 days (year/five years/10 years/life)
        that would make a
    50 percent difference,
    what would I do? *(from Steve Douglass)*

- If I could accomplish only one measurable and strategic thing in the next year, what would I do?

- If I had all of the money, staff, and education I needed, and if knew I could not fail, what would I do?

- What are the strategic things still on my life bucket list?

- What are three key *roles* I want to play well?

- What are three measurable things I want to *do*?

- What are three measurable things I want to *have*?

- What are three people/organizations/causes I want to *help*?

- What are three things I want to leave in my *legacy*?

- What protégés (choose one to three) would I most like to help reach full potential in life?

- If I could solve three strategic problems, what would they be?

- Who is the one person who could still be my mentor and accelerate my lifework?

MOVING FROM "FULL SPEED" TO "SEMI-RETIREMENT"

In our 60s, we also begin thinking about time differently.

Until our 60s, we think in the past: How old am I? How long have I lived?

Beyond our 60s, we switch to thinking about time in the future: How long do I have to live?

Moving from our birth to moving toward age 100 and beyond! "When are you going to retire?"

This is likely one of the most frequently asked questions you are experiencing between the ages of 60 and 70. The question starts even before the day you hit "the big 6-0" and doesn't stop until you say you have.

A majority of adults are pressured into the idea that 65 is the tipping point where all successful people should "be able to retire" or "should retire" or "need to retire" or "should want to retire"!

Let's stop here for just a few minutes and look at the concept of retirement.

When I was about 19 years old, I saw a sign that read,

> **An activity is work
> only if you would rather be doing
> something else!**

Many people would far rather work somewhere other
than where they are working, but they have to keep
doing the work to make a living for their family. They
have to go to work every day.

Like many others — hopefully including you — I
"get" to consult, and fortunately people pay me to do
what I really enjoy doing! I can't think of anything I'd
rather do to make a living than what I do: consulting,
writing, and speaking. By the above definition I
stopped working and "retired" at age 34!

You may not want to retire because you do not want
to stop doing what you want/get to do. Retiring
would mean you would need to stop doing what
you enjoy and start doing what you don't really want
to do: sit around the house all day or play golf, go
fishing, or hang out at the senior center all day.

In my experience, most successful executives today
express sentiments like this on their 65th birthday:
"Things are finally coming together with my
company/organization/church, with our team, with
our working capital, and our credibility."

At age 65, my clients have typically felt, "I'm just really getting started!" Most of my clients really enjoy working until they are at least 75!

If you, for whatever reason, are beginning to look at moving from working harder than you did at age 35 to stopping cold turkey and retiring, consider this word of warning:

> Move from full speed to semi-retirement;
> do not
> quit cold turkey and retire.

Months before you plan to announce that you are moving into semi-retirement, you may want to begin writing down what nonwork activities you will be doing at the same time you are still working — at what you really enjoy doing.

So many quit work cold turkey to retire and then experience a feeling of being emotionally lost for a year or two. They feel totally disoriented. They go from having a well-respected title to no title at all.

As my friend Tom Shrader used to say,

> *"It doesn't take long to move from Who's Who*
> *to*
> *'Who's he/she?'"*

You are maximizing your strategic 60s by
FOCUSING ON STRATEGIC BOULDERS.

WHERE DO I GO FROM HERE?

If you are like most readers, you skipped chapters to quickly learn about your current decade. That's fine!

Does what you have read "hit the nail on the head," as most readers say?
If it does, where do you go from here?

May I suggest one of five steps:

1. Read the *rest* of the book
   ... to anticipate more and more of your own future.

2. Read *earlier* chapters
   ... to better understand what your children and protégés are feeling.

3. Read about a decade someone you care *about* is in today
   ... to help you better understand her/his current phase of life.

4. Read and *give* your book to a family member or friend
   ... to help them better understand their life

situation at this time.

5. **Read and file this book in your personal library**
   ... to reread when you get to each of your next decades.

You
are in a very different phase of life today
than you were 10 years ago
or will be 10 years from now!

Happy to get a few pages to think with you about this
phase of your life!

Bobb

Chapter 8: **70s**

Word of the decade:
SUCCESSION

Unconscious, emotionally disturbing question of the decade:

WHO WILL CARRY ON WHAT I'VE BEEN DOING?

MENTORING YOUR SUCCESSORS: A SIGNIFICANT PART OF YOUR LEGACY

You have worked hard for a lifetime to build up what you have in life. Who will take it over when you are no longer able to manage it or if you are disabled by an accident? Be sure to select your successor very carefully. That process may take two to 10 years. It needs to start in your 70s if it hasn't started earlier.

As defined earlier:

> Ideally,
> mentoring is a lifelong relationship
> in which a mentor helps a protégé reach their
> God-given potential.

Once you decide who your successor will be, try seeing yourself as their mentor — not their manager.

Continue asking these two mentoring questions:

1. What are your plans?
2. How can I help?

Your mentoring relationship can continue until you are 100 or older, long after you no longer work at the organization!

This is also a great time of life to mentor young people who are outside of your work — i.e., not your successors. As I mentioned earlier, I try to ask every young leader in their 30s,

> "Who are the two or three wisest people you know personally — people you like, believe in, and look up to?"

It is time for you to actually reverse the question. Ask yourself,

> "Who are the two or three highest-potential

young people I know personally — people I like, believe in, and would be honored to help along in life?"

Take them to breakfast or lunch and ask about their plans and how you may be of help.

Your young protégés are going to run into a lot of situations where they are going to need your experience and wisdom.

As I wrote earlier, it's shocking how many young leaders in their 30s don't have a parent they feel they can go to for wise counsel.

WRITING OUT YOUR MEMORIES FOR THE NEXT 10 GENERATIONS OF YOUR FAMILY

If you had a few pages of handwritten memories and/ or advice written by your great-great-great-great-great-grandfather or -grandmother in 1694, 1732, 1864 or 1929, would you read it at least once in your life?

What memories would you share with the next 10 generations of your family, if you could sit down by the fire and speak with them personally? What advice would you give?

I wrote a book called *Memories* (see BobbBiehl.com), which Focus on the Family has featured many times on its international radio broadcast. The *Memories* book encourages you to write out your memories for several reasons:

1. There aren't that many hours you get with your children, grandchildren, great-grandchildren, nieces, and nephews, particularly if they live hundreds or thousands of miles away.

2. Your life experience and advice needs to be written out, not only for your child or grandchild, but for 10 generations of your family. You can be assured whatever you write out by hand, and keep as a family legacy, will be read by every one of your descendants for the next 10 generations.

3. This is a great way to pass any of your valued family traditions to others.

4. By doing this, you can be reasonably certain that each of your descendants will know of your spiritual perspectives and other life values.

So the question becomes this when you're in your 70s: What do you want to communicate to the next 10 generations of your extended family?

START TODAY!

KEEPING YOUR WILL UPDATED

Do not delay updating your will just because you don't know precisely how to answer certain questions at this point in your life. Having 70 to 80 percent of your will like you want it is far better than having zero percent of it completed. Trusted estate attorneys are experienced in helping you sort out life's tougher questions.

Also, as you enter your 70s you are becoming progressively aware of your health; in the early 70s it seems like every ache and pain could be something serious. Make sure you have reliable healthcare available

You are maximizing your life contribution
by
PREPARING YOUR SUCCESSORS:
    family, work associates, and protégés!

WHERE DO I GO FROM HERE?

If you are like most readers, you skipped chapters to quickly learn about your current decade. That's fine!

Does what you have read "hit the nail on the head," as most readers say? If it does, where do you go from here?

May I suggest one of five steps:

1. **Read the *rest* of the book**
   ... to anticipate more and more of your own future.

2. **Read *earlier* chapters**
   ... to better understand what your children and protégés are feeling.

3. **Read about a decade someone you care *about* is in today**
   ... to help you better understand her/his current phase of life.

4. **Read and *give* your book to a family member or friend**
   ... to help them better understand their life situation at this time.

5. **Read and file this book in your personal *library***
   ... to reread when you get to each of your next decades.

You are in a very different phase of life today than you were 10 years ago or will be 10 years from now!

Happy to get a few pages to think with you about this phase of your life!

Bobb

Chapter 9: **80s**

Word of the decade:

Slippery

Unconscious, emotionally disturbing question of the decade:

CAN I COUNT ON MY HEALTH?

KEEPING UP YOUR HEALTH BECOMES A REGULAR ROUTINE

Our 80s is a decade where we need to be more careful than in previous decades. In our 80s we need to "salt the ice." If we carefully salt the ice, and have a body to sustain us, we still have much to offer.

Jack is now 82, and he works with organic farming and processing inspections. He just got a five-year government contract. He is having a great time. Jack still has much to offer and is living large.

Your 80s is a decade when you have the time to really relax as you have hoped to do for years.

Your 80s is a decade when you can semi-retire or retire

at a deeper level than in your 60s or 70s.

Your 80s is a decade when you have time to be parents, grandparents, and/or great-grandparents at the level you have been desiring.

Keep your health!
Enjoy your 80s!

ATTENDING FRIENDS' FUNERALS: SUPPORTING THEIR FAMILY MEMBERS

Life now is slippery. Friends and peers are having serious, unpredictable health problems. More and more of them, even those much younger than you, have already died of a wide variety of unexpected major health issues. Life doesn't last forever. When you're 30, you think life lasts forever. By the time you hit your 80s, you are realizing it does not.

One option you may consider after attending a friend's funeral is to, in some way, help your friend's family. Care in some way for a spouse, a family member, or perhaps provide financial counsel. Ask yourself: How can I help support the family of my departed friend as I would like them to care for mine?

REDUCING YOUR EXPENSES
TO A "NEW NORMAL"

Your 80s is a decade when financial concerns can go
one of two ways:

Too much money:
>   How do I divide it up fairly and strategically when
>   I die?

You may have far more money than you want to leave
to children and/or grandchildren; you may fear too
much money will spoil children, turning them into
"trust fund kids." You do not want the anticipation
of receiving a large inheritance to make your children
lazy as they "wait for Dad and Mom to die."

You do not want to leave so much it takes all of the
earning incentive out of living for their children
or grandchildren. This is where the question often
becomes, "How much do we leave the children, and
how much do we leave to our favorite charities?"

It may also be very difficult to figure out "who gets
what part of our estate" when we pass away. This is
very complicated with many children, grandchildren,
great-grandchildren and, in many situations, two,
three, or four families involved, as the result of divorce
and remarriage.

Consider giving each of your family members a
set amount and your favorite charities a certain

percentage of whatever is left.

Not enough money:

Do I have enough to provide adequately until
I go?

However, this is also a decade when, for you, finances
may be very limited.

There is an old saying:

When your outgo
exceeds your income
your upkeep
will be your downfall.

Your 80s is a good time to downsize to a smaller
home, a smaller car, and less spending. Establish a
"new normal" for spending.

There is also the matter of where you will live in the
next few years. Should you move into a smaller place?
What will you do with all of the things you have
accumulated? When and where do you move? Near
the "kids"? Should you move into senior housing?
These decisions are never easy.

If you are ever planning to move, however, now is
the time — before your energy sags and you simply
do not have the time or (sometimes) money to move
where you really want to. Do not count on natural
energy to make such a move in your 90s. Every day

you wait, it gets harder!

Then there is the issue of "Where will we be buried?" Many couples have lived in many locations and their children are spread from "here to there." A century ago, families tended to stay in one location, raise their children in one location, die in one location, and be buried in one location. Not so today. Now is the time to discuss final preparations carefully with your spouse and/or family.

In your 80s
you are still offering life much,
if you are KEEPING YOUR HEALTH!

WHERE DO I GO FROM HERE?

If you are like most readers, you skipped chapters to quickly learn about your current decade. That's fine!

Does what you have read "hit the nail on the head," as most readers say?
If it does, where do you go from here?

May I suggest one of five steps:

1. Read the *rest* of the book
... *to anticipate more and more of your own*
future.

2. **Read *earlier* chapters**
   ... to better understand what your children and protégés are feeling.

3. **Read about a decade someone you care *about* is in today**
   ... to help you better understand her/his current phase of life.

4. **Read and *give* your book to a family member or friend**
   ... to help them better understand their life situation at this time.

5. **Read and file this book in your personal *library***
   ... to reread when you get to each of your next decades.

You
are in a very different phase of life today
than you were 10 years ago
or will be 10 years from now!

Happy to get a few pages to think with you about this phase of your life!

Bobb

CHAPTER 10: **90S-PLUS**

Word of the decade:

Sleep

Unconscious, emotionally disturbing question of the decade:

HOW LONG BEFORE I GET TO SLEEP?

TELLING YOUR NEW YOUNG FRIENDS TO CALL YOU BY YOUR FIRST NAME

Younger people think of you as "older."

You think of younger people over 30 simply as "adults."

Does that shock you? It's true. Ask yourself: Do you think of anyone over 30 who is younger than you as "younger," or do you simply think of them as "adults"?

Do you think of anyone 10 years older than you as "older"?

Can you imagine how few people see you as peers?

Young people see you as an "old person" who deserves the respect of being called "Mr. Smith," "Grandma," or "Ma'am/Sir."

You need to give them permission to call you by your first name. Permission to see you as a friend, not a "highly respected" older person.

This poem captures the essence of the point I'm trying to make.

MINNIE REMEMBERS

God,
my hands are old.
I've never said that out loud before,
but they are.

I was so proud of them once.
They were soft
like the velvet smoothness
of a firm, ripe peach.

Now the softness is more like
worn-out sheets
or withered leaves.

When did these slender,
graceful hands become
gnarled, shrunken claws?

When, God?
They lie here in my lap,
naked reminders of this
worn-out body that has
served me too well.

How long has it been since
someone touched me?
Twenty years?
Twenty years I've been a widow.

Respected,
Smiled at, but never touched.

Never held so close that loneliness
was blotted out.

I remember how my mother used to hold me,
God. When I was hurt in spirit or flesh,
she would gather me close,
stroke my silky hair,
and caress my back
with her warm hands.

O God, I'm so lonely!

I remember the first boy
who ever kissed me.
We were both so new at that!

The taste of young lips and popcorn,
the feeling inside of mysteries

to come.

I remember Hank and the babies.

How else can I remember them
but together?
Out of the fumbling, awkward
attempts of new lovers
came the babies.

And as they grew, so did our love.
And, God, Hank didn't seem to mind if my
body thickened and faded
a little.

He still loved it.
And touched it.
And we didn't mind if we were
no longer beautiful.
And it felt so good.
And the children hugged me a lot.

O God, I'm so lonely!

God, why didn't we raise the kids
to be silly and affectionate
as well as dignified and proper?

You see, they do their duty.
They drive up in their fine cars;
they come to my room to pay their respects.

They chatter brightly and reminisce.

But they don't touch me.

They call me "Mom" or "Mother"
or "Grandma."
Never Minnie. My mother called me Minnie.
So did my friends. Hank called me Minnie, too.
But they're gone.
And so is Minnie.
Only Grandma is here.

And God, she's lonely!

"Touch Them Gently" by Donna Swanson

Once again, you need to give them permission to call you by your first name — permission to see you as a friend, not a "highly respected" older person.

SELECTING AN ADVOCATE

Today, you may be experiencing a considerable lack of energy, requiring a walking stick or walker, needing state-of-the-art hearing aids, driving only short distances (if you are driving at all), and needing a considerable amount of assistance in general.

You may need help in making all of your doctor appointments, caring for your personal needs, and managing all of your financial affairs. You may need an advocate.

Proud as you may have been in your earlier phase of life, you need an advocate to protect you in life's push-push-push pace and complex bureaucratic systems.

Also, always welcome a helper, be it a relative or perfect stranger, even if only for 10 minutes, especially when you are at a frustrating vending machine that doesn't work or a ramp that a self-powered wheelchair won't climb.

Hopefully, you are looking back over your life and embracing what may be your last decade. Hopefully, the 90s come after you have resolved your estate situation and come to terms with your legacy, although you may be dealing with health diagnoses. Many in their 90s embrace this decade, some against incredible odds!

A world-renowned geriatric psychiatrist tells his 90-year-old patients to push themselves and get up and out of bed. He knows from his practice that once a person in this age group just stays in bed sleeping, he or she will often stay in bed and not get up. He actually says, "Push yourself!" His patients in their 90s often get up immediately — no matter the pain.

It can make a life-changing difference, even to someone who is already full of life!

GOING TO "SLEEP" IN PEACE: PREPARING FOR YOUR OWN PASSING

One of the most common expressions I have heard from those in their 90s is, "I don't want to die the way I saw my parents die in a nursing home! I just want to go to sleep and wake up in heaven and be with my departed loved ones."

Today, you may be facing death eye to eye within a very short period of time. You may be asking, like so many do, "How can I know I'm going to heaven when I die?"

I'm not a biblical scholar and I'm not a cleric. So I asked a trusted friend of mine to give me a clear and simple answer to this question I could share with friends.

This was his response.

You can KNOW you are going
to heaven
when you die!

From my earliest childhood — in fact, beginning nine months before I was born! — I went to church. Yet the answer to where I would spend eternity somehow escaped me. Instead, an almost

---

paralyzing fear of death gripped my heart.

One night I dreamt that a tidal wave swept my family out to sea and I was drowning. Just as I went down for the final time, I awakened in a cold sweat and thought, "I'm not ready for eternity!"

Another time I was traveling aboard a troopship, when suddenly a siren blasted a warning that the ship was sinking. Everyone donned their life jackets and ran for the lifeboats. My heart almost stopped, for fear of where I was really headed! But thankfully, I learned that it was just a fire drill.

Years later these fearful episodes ended, when someone told me that I didn't have to wonder about my final destination; that it is possible to know for certain that I will spend eternity with God in heaven! Acting on that news changed my life. The fear was gone, and in its place were joy, peace and courage in the face of death. Best of all, I had a deep assurance that I would spend eternity with God in heaven.

Let me ask you a couple of questions.

- Do you know for certain where you will spend eternity?

- Will it be in heaven?

- What would you say if God were to ask you, "Why should I let you into my heaven?"

If you are unsure, or hesitate for even a moment in answering these questions, the few minutes it will take you to read the good news I'd like to share with you can make all the difference in your future! God says in his Word, the Holy Bible, "I write these things to you … that you may know that you have eternal life." (See 1 John 5:13.) How can we know that?

Heaven is a free gift

The Bible tells us, "The gift of God is eternal life." (See Romans 6:23.) This is good news! A true gift is freely given and freely received. In this case, eternal life is freely given by God and can be freely received by us or anyone, no matter who you are or what you've done. Heaven is not earned or deserved by us, because everyone sins. The Bible says, "All have sinned and fall short of the glory of God." (See Romans 3:23.) Sin is breaking God's law, and includes lying, cheating, deceit, stealing, evil thoughts, and immoral behavior, among other things.

Have you ever wondered just how good you would have to be to make it to heaven? God said, "Be perfect therefore, just as your heavenly Father is perfect." (See Matthew 5:48.) Since it is impossible to be perfect, even the smallest sin disqualifies us from heaven. We can't be good enough, so there must be an entirely different way to get there!

God is merciful and does not want to punish us. He says, "I have loved you with an everlasting love." (See Jeremiah 31:3.) But the same Bible that tells us that God loves us also tells us that God is perfectly just. So He must punish sin. He "does not leave the guilty unpunished." (See Exodus 34:7b.)

God solved this problem in the person of Jesus Christ. Who would you say Jesus is? The Bible teaches that Jesus is God. Anyone who wants to know what God is like can find out from the perfect and sinless life of Jesus. He died on the cross and rose from the dead to pay the penalty for our sins, and to purchase a place for us in heaven, which He offers as a free gift. Does everyone receive this gift? No.

This gift is received by faith. Faith is the key

that opens the door to eternal life in heaven. It is not a blind leap in the dark. It is not just head knowledge. Nor is it just a temporary belief. Saving faith is trusting in Jesus Christ alone as rescuer for eternal life. It means believing in Jesus alone, and in what He has done, rather than anything we can do for ourselves to gain heaven. "For God so loved the world that He gave His only Son, that whoever believes in Him shall not perish but have eternal life." (See John 3:16.)

Would you like to receive God's gift of eternal life? Because this is so important, let's clarify what it involves.

Trust Him

It means you accept Christ as your Savior. Open the door to your life and invite Him in. He says, "I stand at the door and knock. If anyone hears my voice and opens the door, I will come in." (See Revelation 3:20.) It means you also need to receive Him as Lord of your life, giving Him the driver's seat of your life, not the back seat.

It means that you need to repent — that is, be willing to turn from anything that is not pleasing to God. He will tell you what He wants you to do as you grow in your relationship with Him, and He will give you the strength to do it.

You can receive this gift of eternal life through Jesus Christ, right where you are. "For it is with your heart that you believe and are justified, and it is with your mouth that you confess and are saved." (See Romans 10:10.)

You can pray right now and receive eternal life. Use your own words to pray, or use this prayer:

> Jesus Christ, I know that I am sinful and do not deserve eternal life.
> I believe you died and rose from the dead to purchase a place in heaven for me.
> Lord, come into my life and take control of my life. Please forgive my sins.
> I confess them, and now believe in You for salvation.
> I accept your free gift of eternal life, and I thank You for it.

If this prayer expresses what you believe in your heart, Jesus promises you this: "I tell you the truth, he who believes has eternal life." NOW YOU CAN KNOW YOU HAVE ETERNAL LIFE. And if you have truly turned away from your sins, placed your trust in Jesus Christ's sacrificial death, and received the gift of eternal life, you are now a child of God! Forever! "Yet all who received Him, to those who believed in

His name, to them He gave the right to become children of God." (See John 1:12.)

You can be sure you are GOING TO HEAVEN.

Welcome to God's family!

So what's next?

- **Read the Bible.**
  Start with the gospel of John. Read a chapter a day. "As newborn babes, desire the pure milk of the word (of God), that you may grow thereby." (See 1 Peter 2:2.) You can access the Bible for free on for your computer or mobile device by visiting Bible.com.

- **Pray.**
  Spend time each day talking with God. "Do not be anxious about anything, but in everything, by prayer and petition, with thanksgiving, present your requests to God." (See Philippians 4:6.)

- **Worship God.**
  Attend a church that teaches the Bible and encourages you to love Him and all people. "God is Spirit, and they that worship Him must worship Him in spirit and in truth." (See John 4:24.)

- **Spend time with other Christians.**
  Christians who will help you grow in the faith. "And they devoted themselves to the apostles' teaching and fellowship, to the breaking of bread and the prayers." (See Acts 2:42.)

- **Tell others what Jesus means to you!**
  "But you will receive power when the Holy Spirit comes on you, and you will be my witnesses." (See Acts 1:8.)

You can be sure you are going to heaven.

—Tom Stebbins

If you or your loved one are in your 90s and fast approaching the end, the following hospice thoughts may be a good guide for bedside conversation or counseling.

HOSPICE THOUGHTS

People are often surprised when I tell them that some of my happiest and most fulfilling years were the years I was a hospice chaplain. In those years I was privileged to talk with patients and families about a lot of things that really mattered. I got to be with them as they took care of unfinished business and got some important things finally nailed down.

I learned from other hospice workers the five things dying patients needed to say before they died. We often saw if they did *not* say these things their dying was more difficult physically, emotionally and spiritually. I witnessed beautiful and healing moments as people in time said the five following things:

1. Forgive me.
2. I forgive you.
3. I love you.
4. Thank you.
5. Goodbye.

Eventually, I saw the need to add a sixth thing needing to be said:

6. I forgive me.

Forgiving oneself was big for many people as they experienced God's forgiveness of them.

I want to so live, so that when it comes time for me to die, all I have to do is die. Frequently saying these six things now helps me to do so. It means not only being ready to die, but being ready to live.

Tim Smith
Fellow Traveler

For more information about hospice, visit:

HospiceFoundation.org

Wrap Up

Decade by decade, life is surprisingly predictable, wouldn't you agree?

Hopefully, as you have read these pages, you have seen that predictability captured in a single S-word. These S-words make it easy for you to capture each decade in your memory. Each word allows you to begin understanding at new levels what to expect in future decades and gain a deeper understanding of past decades.

Understanding the phase of life you are in — and seeing that you are not alone in what you are experiencing — helps you relax at a very deep level.

> With predictability comes a deeper confidence in living life!
>
> With predictability comes a deeper confidence in helping friends!
>
> With predictability comes a deeper confidence in relaxing!

As I said in the introduction:

> The observations and perspectives in this book strike most people as very good news. You will

find in it fresh, healthy, encouraging perspectives. Hopefully, you will be helping a friend with these ideas before this week (or day) has ended.

Here to help you turn your dreams into reality,

Bobb

An introduction ... and an invitation!

As an executive mentor/consultant, I have the rare privilege of spending days at a time with some of the finest leaders of our generation. I continue to grow personally, learning more in the past year than I've learned in the five years before it.

Mentoring Realities

As you now know, I define mentoring as, ideally, "a lifelong relationship in which the mentor helps the protégé grow into their God-given potential over a lifetime." Realistically, because of schedule pressures, my personal mentoring is limited to a very few individuals. At the same time, I truly want to see friends like you grow into your God-given potential over your lifetime.

Solomon advised, "Get wisdom."

The search of today seems to be focused on becoming a courageous, charming, powerful, successful person. However, according to the Bible, Solomon, who was one of the wisest, if not the wisest, man that ever lived, gave us this profound and timeless bit of advice in Proverbs 4:5: GET WISDOM!

This is advice that our modern world seems to overlook. Enter the idea of **Quick Wisdom**.

The focus of **Quick Wisdom** is to help you and your friends be WISE!

Today, it seems that every young leader I meet wants wisdom, but needs it fast. We don't have the time with today's pace and pressures to go to a mountaintop and study ancient manuscripts in Sanskrit. Thus my idea for quick access to timeless wisdom. My focus: weekly, I will send **Quick Wisdom** emails for you to read and pass on with the very best "wisdom nuggets" I can give you to help strengthen your protégés and friends.

Quick Wisdom is 100 percent free to you and your friends.

Fortunately, the email technology of today is such that you can enroll 10 friends or 100 to receive the Quick Wisdom email. It takes me the same amount of time to send you an email as it does to send it to all of your protégés and/or friends. I want to use my unique exposure to great wisdom to strengthen you and your friends for a lifetime.

Thank you, my friend, for telling your friends about **Quick Wisdom!**

To receive these FREE **Quick Wisdom** emails, simply visit BobbBiehl.com and sign up.

Helping you ...

... your children, your protégés and your staff — no matter what you do, no matter where you go, for the rest of your life — is the reason the following tools exist.

These tools are presented in five categories, each with five top tools:
   A. PERSONAL DEVELOPMENT
   B. LEADERSHIP DEVELOPMENT
   C. ORGANIZATIONAL DEVELOPMENT
   D. PLANNING
   E. GIFTS

A. PERSONAL DEVELOPMENT

1. NORTH STAR (video)
   Focusing your life — and keeping it focused.

   Focusing your next 50 years at the 50,000-foot level, in less than 50 minutes. Once focused, it is easy to refocus your life in a matter of minutes.

2. BUCKET LIST (video)
   Focusing your future — and keeping it in focus.

   What are the few measurable things you really want to get done — before you die? This is your

Bucket List! This one video helps you create your personal bucket list in a very short period of time.

3. 4TH-GRADE(R) (book or video)
   Life's turning point.

   Fourth grade, age 9, is the single most shaping year of a person's existence. This DVD explains how your fourth grade shaped your life, or that of the staff member you are about to hire.

4. WHY YOU DO WHAT YOU DO (book)
   Understanding yourself and others.

   This book is a result of more than 50,000 hours of behind-the-smiles experiences with some of the finest leaders of our generation. It can help you better understand your spouse, your family members, and your team members.

5. DECADE BY DECADE (book)
   Life is surprisingly predictable.

   This book gives you a decade-by-decade understanding of what is "normal" for each decade of life, based on observing over 5,000 people personally over the last 45-plus years. This understanding helps bring perspective to what you are dealing with today.

B. LEADERSHIP DEVELOPMENT

6. ASKING PROFOUND QUESTIONS (booklet)
   Getting to the heart of an issue — fast!

   This confidence-building booklet contains more
   than 100 profound questions to help you deal
   effectively with life 24 hours a day, seven days a
   week, for the rest of your life.

7. ANNUAL BALANCE CALENDAR (video)
   Balancing your life, personal and professional.

   This one simple DVD helps you find and keep
   far more balance between your personal and your
   professional life! Once your life is in balance, you
   have a clear context for daily, weekly, monthly,
   and quarterly effectiveness.

8. LEADING WITH CONFIDENCE (book)
   For the rest of your life.

   A wise, proven investment in your own future,
   covering 30 essential leadership areas, including:

   HOW TO COPE WITH change, depression,
   failure, fatigue, and pressure.

   HOW TO BECOME MORE attractive,
   balanced, confident, creative, disciplined, and
   motivated.

HOW TO DEVELOP SKILLS IN asking, dreaming, goal setting, prioritizing, risk taking, influencing, money managing, personal organization, problem solving, decision making, and communicating.

HOW TO BECOME MORE EFFECTIVE IN delegating, firing, reporting, team building, people building, recruiting, strategic planning, and motivating.

9. LEADERSHIP ACADEMY (24-DVD series)

    Proven at all levels.

    This series (24 DVDs and an accompanying series of handouts in a notebook) is the essence of the leadership tools, processes, and principles every leader needs, at all levels of leadership. These tools are scalable from the smallest startup group up to the president of any nation. This material comes from 45-plus years and thousands of hours of consulting with over 500 organizations. These DVDs will help strengthen you as a leader — for the rest of your life!

10. MENTORING (book)
    How to find a mentor and how to become one.

    If you would like to find a mentor or become a mentor but don't know where to start, this is the place! This book explains clearly what mentoring is, what mentors do and don't do, the nature of the mentor-protégé relationship, the most common roadblocks to effective mentoring, and much more.

ORGANIZATIONAL DEVELOPMENT

11. BOARDROOM CONFIDENCE (book)
First board or 10th board.

If you are considering serving on a board, are already on a board, or are the chairperson leading a board, *Boardroom Confidence* is a valuable and proven tool to help you and your board serve with confidence!

12. OPPORTUNITY-SPOTTING QUESTIONS (video)
Opportunity – key to explosive growth!

Opportunity-Spotting Questions is a shockingly simple series of profound questions that can help you spot high-potential opportunities everyone on your team — including you — is overlooking.

13. STOP SETTING GOALS (book)
   If you prefer solving problems!

   Within 100 miles of you at this moment:
   approximately 15 percent of adults are naturally
   energized by GOALS! Approximately 80
   percent are naturally energized by PROBLEMS!
   Approximately five percent are naturally energized
   by OPPORTUNITIES!

   This insight is a critical understanding for anyone
   in any leadership or management position who
   is responsible for motivating and maximizing a
   team.

14. TEAM PROFILE (self-scoring inventory)
   Getting "round pegs in round holes."

   The *Team Profile* lets you tell others:

   > What makes you tick!
   > What turns you on!
   > What burns you out!

   It helps each team member define her or his
   ideal role on the team and is key to building a
   successful team. It helps you get "round pegs in
   round holes."

15. FIRING STAR (video)
    Firing a team member — in a "Christian way."

    Firing Star helps you release a staff person in a
    humane way. The way in which they are released
    makes a huge difference. *Firing Star* helps you
    know how to release a person in the way you
    would want to be released!

PLANNING

16. STRATEGIC PLANNING ARROW
    (24" x 36" sheet)
    Your team's future direction, on one sheet of paper.

    The *Strategic Planning Arrow* is a proven tool for
    helping teams define a clear team direction. When
    a team is making the same basic assumptions
    about direction, it dramatically reduces the
    frustration, pressure, and tension the team is
    experiencing on a day-to-day basis! (Formerly
    titled: "Masterplanning Arrow.")

17. STRATEGIC PLANNING (book)
    Step-by-step planning process.

    By reading one book, your whole team can have
    one proven, step-by-step planning process they
    all understand, regardless of background. Proven

in hundreds of organizations, divisions, and departments with a wide variety of leadership styles. (Formerly titled: "Masterplanning.")

18. SPEED PLANNING (video)
When you have one to three planning hours, not one to three days.

Whenever you are running short on time but still need to focus your team, this is a very helpful tool. It doesn't help you put together a 30-page plan, but it quickly gives your team focus on a couple of sheets.

19. VITAL SIGNS AND CRITICAL STANDARDS (video)
Keeping your organization healthy.

The *Vital Signs and Critical Standards* video helps you quickly tell if your organization is healthy, if you should be concerned, or if your organization is in real trouble! At your option, you can also give these charts to your board, reassuring them or alerting them to major problems.

20. PROCESS CHARTING (video)
Key to transferability.

When any responsibility, program, or

organization is transferred from one person
to the next, process is the secret of effectively
transferring the responsibility.

GIFTS

21. ON MY OWN (book)
     Perfect gift for graduation.

     If you have been increasingly concerned about
     your high school or college student's readiness to
     face the "real world," this book has been written
     for the students in your world. These principles
     will stay with them for a lifetime, and they can
     pass them on to their children's children.

22. LEADERSHIP INSIGHTS (book)
     Perfect gift for young executives.

     Leadership Insights contains the 101 insights,
     principles, definitions, and rules of thumb that
     can help you in any type of work — for the rest
     of your life!

23. DATING QUESTIONS (book)
     Perfect gift for couples beginning to date seriously.

     This gift book teaches any young couple 250 fun

questions to ask BEFORE they get engaged or married. It will help both of them know the real person "behind the smile" — before asking "Will you?" or answering "I will!" (Formerly titled: "Should We Get Married?")

24. HEAVEN (book)
Perfect gift for hospice care or grieving.

Heaven gives deep comfort to any person facing imminent death or grieving the loss of a loved one. Reading *Heaven* helps a person imagine what heaven could be like in a vivid, inviting, and comforting way.

25. MEMORIES (album-/heirloom-type books)
Perfect gift for parents or grandparents.

The *Memories* book contains 500-plus memory-jogging questions to help your loved one remember and write about her or his life experiences. It's a beautiful album-type book with padded covers and a binding that opens widely for easy writing. It's a great birthday or Christmas gift for any living parent, grandparent, aunt, uncle, or mentor!

Helping you continue
growing into your full potential
and
building your family or team
is the reason each of these tools exist.

They are all available at BobbBiehl.com.

Here to help turn your dreams into reality,

Bobb

Bobb Biehl
Coach, Consultant, Executive Mentor

Coach — Teaching specific skills.
Consultant — Helping leaders build organizations.
Executive Mentor — A lifelong relationship, helping
an executive you believe in reach their God-given
potential.